THE CULINARY CYCLIST

A Cookbook and Companion for the Good Life

Anna Brones

illustrated by Johanna Kindvall

The Culinary Cyclist
A Cookbook and Companion for the Good Life

Text and recipes © 2013, 2015 by Anna Brones
Illustrations © 2013, 2015 Johanna Kindvall

Cover design by Joe Biel

This edition © Elly Blue Publishing, an imprint of Microcosm Publishing, 2015

Second Edition, September 15, 2015
ISBN 978-1-62106-825-9

Distributed by Legato / Perseus + Turnaround (UK)

Printed on post-consumer paper in the U.S.

Find more feminist bicycle books and other titles at EllyBluePublishing.com

Microcosm Publishing
2752 N Williams Ave.
Portland, OR 97227
TakingTheLane.com
MicrocosmPublishing.com

CONTENTS

INTRODUCTION

On a bicycle, there is freedom in propelling yourself forward. You are rewarded for your output, and even the shortest ride provides a sense of accomplishment. The bicycle is empowering.

Food is the same. There is joy in a dinner made from scratch—as much as or more than the one served at a fancy restaurant. Both on the bicycle and in the kitchen, hard labor pays off. "I can make that" is just as powerful as "I can ride that."

Just as communities form around different aspects of bicycling, food is a uniting force. We gather, we talk, we laugh and we break bread together. So it makes perfect sense to combine the two into this book; a guide to good living, with food, by bicycle.

The rules for living well, if you can call them that, are simple and a pleasure to follow. Eat local and mostly plants. Ride your bike, even on rainy days. Say yes to dinner invitations. Always bring your signature dessert. Invite people on picnics. Bike in the sunshine. Follow a morning ride with a strong French press.

This might all sound like a utopian hipster dream, but the bicycle and food are two of the simplest things we have at our disposal. Unfortunately we live in a culture where honoring the two has taken on a certain level of pretentiousness; committing to healthy eating habits and a two-wheeled lifestyle are often devalued in the face of speed and stress. Driving and fast food are so ubiquitous that we don't even see them, even when we are wondering how to achieve the good life.

I grew up with a Swedish mother, and her European sensibility formed a large part of my upbringing. My father was the cycling enthusiast. Throughout my childhood we explored together on a tandem. As I have traveled to Sweden as an adult, the difference in bike cultures has always struck me.

Infrastructure in Sweden supports a two-wheeled lifestyle and in turn, cycling in Sweden is simply part of a lifestyle.

The way that some of us in bike-centric capitals like Brooklyn or Portland can wax ecstatic about how obsessed we are with our bicycles simply wouldn't happen there. In Sweden, you own a bicycle, it's probably an old and heavy single speed, and it gets you from point A to point B—it's so normal that you don't even think about it.

Eating good, simple food is a given in the same way. Until I became an adult, I wasn't even conscious of the fact that I ate "healthy food." It was simply something that we did. My mother always had me helping in the kitchen, putting together whole grains and fresh ingredients. There wasn't a microwave in sight.

In the modern age, we like to overcomplicate things. That's why riding a bicycle brings joy: it's simple. Simple food is the same, but in a world of corporate agribusiness, we have been brainwashed by food marketing to the point that we often put into question people that eat well. But cooking your own lentils and sauteeing chard shouldn't be trendy, it should just be normal. It's the fast food hamburger that we should be questioning.

Not all of us have the luxury of choice. For those of us who do, thinking about what we eat isn't an option, it's an obligation. Good food doesn't have to be complicated, and it certainly doesn't have to be pretentious.

Just like you once mastered two wheels, this book helps you master food, while making it easy, fun and as sustainable as humanly possible. Think of this as a vehicle for thinking about what you eat, as well as for enjoying it and finding pleasure in the smallest culinary tasks.

A bike ride can take you around the block or across the country. A meal can do the same. Put the two together? Now that's a formula for living well.

single speed

americano

internet device

cruiser

hot sauce

cilantro

fish

pickled onions

cyclocross

blue berries

banana

oatmeal

A NOTE ON DIETARY RESTRICTIONS

When I was 17, my mother learned she was gluten intolerant. This was before the gluten-free rage, and cutting out pasta and other starches was certainly not the norm. Never diagnosed as gluten intolerant myself, over the years I have learned that I personally feel better not eating gluten. Sure, there is the occasional pizza and microbrew, but for the most part I stick to a gluten-free diet. Over the past two decades I have developed my own food regimen. I couldn't write a book about it, because it's not strictly one thing or another, but it works for me. It's one that is often vegan, but also includes eggs—from happy chickens, of course. It's often dairy free but I do like a good cappuccino. And it's predominantly gluten-free, but if I am at a French bakery you can be sure that I will succumb to a pain aux raisins.

I write this partly as a caveat—all of the recipes in this book are gluten-free—but also as a source of inspiration. Figure out what makes you feel good. Make the recipes that work for you. Tweak the ones that don't. Food is fun, and we all have to figure out the best formula for ourselves. Fad diets and food regimes will always exist, but if you have the personal discipline to eat in moderation and the interest in exploring food, eventually you will settle on a food policy that works for you.

Speaking of food policy, that quinoa didn't exactly come from your backyard. How do we get around the dilemma of consuming foods grown far away?

When it comes to eating more sustainably, this is again about finding a personal food policy. For me it includes buying locally cultivated wine whenever possible, not buying asparagus out of season, and really paying attention to where things come from. Yes I buy quinoa, and yes I buy avocados. But in moderation.

We should vote with our fork, but we should also pick our battles. Be smart about what you buy, but don't lose your mind on account of it. Are you going to stop drinking coffee because it wasn't grown down the street? If you are really committed and can go that far, more power to you, but for the rest of us, accept that we live in a globalized world and some of our habits depend on buying out of our region. So be conscious about this fact and make the best of the situation. Buy from companies that you know treat their workers and the environment in a good way, try to buy produce that's in season, and if something seems too cheap to be true, it probably is.

Food is a celebration. Don't be afraid to indulge once in awhile.

WHY THIS BOOK?

Living well is not just for the one percent; it's something that we can all engage in. It doesn't have to be about nibbling on caviar and washing it down with bubbly (although I'd never turn down an evening of that). It's simply about living intentionally, thinking about how we do things, and constantly improving them. Isn't that why you ride a bicycle? It improves your commute by giving you access to fresh air. It makes the world a better place by reducing your overall impact. It improves your relationships by providing a way to spend time relaxing together.

Food is the same. If we eat better, we live better. We're healthier, and so is our planet.

This guidebook is for navigating those waters. Realizing that what we eat, how we prepare it and who we eat it with is an all encompassing experience, one that brings joy and allows us to celebrate the everyday.

Nietzsche said, "A small garden, figs, a little cheese, and, along with this, three or four good friends—such was luxury to

Epicurus." Add a bicycle to that, and isn't that the definition of the good life?

This book is laid out to help you navigate through the day, starting with breakfast and ending with the after dinner cup of tea. Along the way we work through stocking your pantry, bulk shopping, and transporting your food on two wheels. It's a book that can be read in one sitting, or picked up and browsed a chapter at a time. The recipes peppered throughout have become staples in my own kitchen, not just because they're delicious, but because they're easy and perfectly transportable on two wheels.

Living well doesn't have to be complicated. In fact, it's much like riding a bike. Once you've mastered the basics, you never turn back.

Let's get started.

THE PLEASURE OF GOOD FOOD

Nothing would be more tiresome than eating and drinking
if God had not made them a pleasure as well as a necessity.
–Voltaire

Nothing compares to the simple pleasure of a bike ride.
–John F. Kennedy

What is good food? We all know we should be eating more vegetables, less meat, and less processed flour. But there's more to food than just nutritional value. Food is a process; a holistic experience. You eat to fuel not only your body, but also your soul. Just like a bike ride can be both a way to exercise and also a way to boost your spirit, food nourishes all parts of our body, physical and mental.

We ride because ultimately we find pleasure in it. Food is different in the sense that if we don't eat, we will eventually perish. But if we have to eat every day, isn't it better to find a sense of pleasure in it?

From the second we take our first sip of coffee in the morning, to the last crumb of dessert at the dinner table, there are moments to be enjoyed throughout the day. If we don't take time to appreciate them, we in turn miss out. Eating well isn't just about choosing the right ingredients, it's about allowing yourself the time to be in the present. Honor the food in front of you. Share with friends. Do more with food than just eat it to survive.

Good food isn't just a combination of kale, carrots and brown rice (although it certainly can be), but an all-around approach to eating well that includes choosing food from the right places, interacting with the producers, taking the time to make it by hand, and sharing it with friends and family. Sometimes that's health food, and sometimes it's not. We have to go beyond the food pyramid, beyond thinking about fats and antioxidants and omega 3s. Because you can try your damndest to eat healthy, but if you're not happy doing it, it isn't helping anyone.

Ultimately, good food isn't about restrictions, it's about the liberty to eat what makes your body feel good, emotionally and physically. Eating is a balance. As Julia Child says, "everything in moderation... including moderation."

Eat well, eat balanced and find pleasure in it. Because there is quite frankly no other way to live.

FOR THE LOVE OF CAFFEINE

I have measured out my life with coffee spoons.
–*T.S. Eliot*

When we think of mornings, we inevitably think of coffee. But coffee isn't just fuel to get your day going, it represents a special moment. A moment where we wrap our hands around a warm cup or carefully lift a delicate espresso mug, take a sip and wait for the gradual spread of energy. We have a love affair with coffee not just because it helps us wake up, but because it's an instant of pure concentration. The rest of the world fades away. Your senses are on hyper alert. You feel like you can do anything.

The key to coffee is appreciation. Not pouring large mug upon large mug of drip (although if you're at a good brunch, you should certainly say yes to a top off) but making time for that precious moment where everything else subsides and our senses are completely attuned to what we are drinking.

After crude oil, coffee is the world's second most common traded commodity, and it's first on the list of agricultural commodities. In the United States alone we consume 150 billion cups of coffee per year. When we talk about food, we often talk about voting with our forks, and if there is one change you should make in your consumption habits to do just that, it's coffee (and chocolate too, for that matter).

Specialty coffee isn't just a matter of craft roasting and selling expensive beans, it's a commitment to an entire process that's currently under threat on a variety of fronts. Climate change is one of the biggest predators, changing growing seasons, harvest yields and the quality of beans that farmers can sell.

In a world of corporate agribusiness, buying good coffee means supporting farmers and their livelihoods as well as a commitment to sustainability. So how do you choose?

Here are three basic certifications for coffee and what they mean:

FAIR TRADE

Fair Trade is a commonly used mechanism for ensuring that farmers around the world are being paid fair wages in good working conditions for commodities ranging from coffee to cane sugar. Fair Trade USA certifies growers and ensures that members who belong are paying the prices directly to growers.

SHADE GROWN

Why do you want to be drinking coffee grown in the shade of a tree canopy? Sun tolerant coffee plants that have been developed over the past several decades are high-yield, but their cultivation practices are often considered unsustainable. Studies have shown that there is a direct correlation between the structural complexity of a coffee plantation and the number of species that it has; the more like a forest, the more biodiversity. The Smithsonian Migratory Bird Center developed the first 100%-organic shade-grown coffee certification, and it means that the plantations where the coffee is grown has the proper amount of biodiversity for migratory bird populations. Choose shade grown coffee and choose a richer ecosystem.

DIRECT TRADE

Direct trade means sourcing directly from coffee farmers, and it is becoming more and more popular amongst independent coffee roasters. It allows the coffee roasters to work with growers from estates, cooperatives and small family farms and to know exactly where all of their coffee comes from; it also means farmers receive a higher price for their beans.

The takeaway? Know your coffee company, know where they grow their beans, how they grow them, and how they work with their farmers. After that, it's all a matter of taste.

Cold Brew Coffee

Ingredients

Coffee + water

Ratios of coffee to water vary, and you can tweak according to how strong you want it. For a 32 ounce French press, I use 4 cups water and about 3/4 cup beans, which is a little less than a 1 part coffee to 4 parts water ratio. If using metric, use 960 milliliters water and 75 grams coffee beans, about a 1 to 13 ratio.

Directions

Grind beans coarsely.

Place grounds in empty French press and fill with cold water. Gently stir with a spoon to mix.

Cover the French press with tinfoil and let steep for about 12 hours at room temperature. It's even better when you let it sit for 24 hours, but that takes some planning.

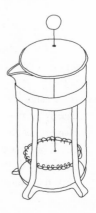

Remove the tinfoil and press the grounds down. Serve over ice. If it's a little strong, dilute with water.

Store in refrigerator in glass bottles or a covered pitcher.

TAKING TIME FOR BREAKFAST

❧⬥❧

We load up on oat bran in the morning so we'll live forever.
Then we spend the rest of the day living like there's no
tomorrow.
–*Lee Iacocca*

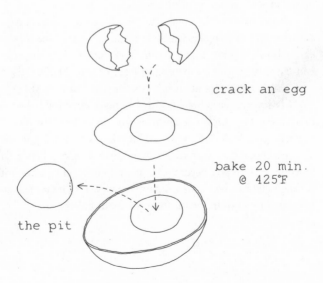

crack an egg

bake 20 min.
@ 425°F

the pit

There is beauty in simplicity, and often enough, that means oatmeal. What's better than a steaming bowl of oats and raisins on a foggy morning on the cyclocross course or before a cold-weather ride to work? But fall into too much of a routine, and breakfast quickly loses its flair.

I don't need to tell you that eating breakfast is important. Why then do so many of us skip out on it? We stayed up way too late the night before, we hit the snooze button a few too many times and now we're sprinting out the door only to pedal as fast as we can so we make it to the office in time. This is no way to live.

Breakfast should be holy. Beyond sustenance, it's a moment to dust out the brain cobwebs leftover from a night of sleep, collect your thoughts and prepare for the day ahead. It's a time to think creatively and reflect peacefully before you launch into a to do list or succumb to checking email.

Part of living well is making time for that moment. A cup of coffee or tea, a piece of homemade bread with jam, a hard boiled egg, a bowl of granola and yogurt. Take equal time to prepare and enjoy what you are putting in front of you. The emails can wait. And you'll certainly feel better on your morning ride.

My favorite easy breakfast that packs a punch is baked egg in avocado. It's simple enough that you can make it for one, but it works just as well to impress your friends at Sunday brunch. The essential two ingredients work like magic when baked together. Above and beyond that, it's a dish to get creative with, adding whatever herbs are on hand, or whatever ingredients are left over in your refrigerator from the night before.

Baked Egg in Avocado

Basic ingredients

1 avocado + 2 eggs (for two servings)
A dash of salt and pepper to taste

Potential topping combinations

Parsley + goat cheese crumbles
Shallots + roquefort cheese
Sauteed mushrooms + chopped basil

Preparation

Preheat oven to 425°F (220°C)

Cut the avocado in half and remove the pit. Scoop out a little of the avocado from the center to make space for the egg. Place avocados in a cast iron skillet or baking pan, making sure they are well propped up and not falling over.

Crack an egg into each avocado half. Depending on the size of your eggs, some of the egg white may spill out. Don't stress about it. For variation, sprinkle in the spices before you put in the egg.

Bake for 20 minutes. This results in the eggs being well done. If you like your eggs a little runnier, reduce the time.

But then there are those mornings when you don't have time for things like baked eggs. The days when you just need to be able to get up and go. No matter the situation, mornings are always our chance to do better. Forget what happened the day before, the second we wake up, we have the chance to start anew.

If you grew up in the United States, you were likely raised in a culture where breakfast meant some sort of starch (a colored one if you were lucky), milk, orange juice and maybe a meat product. You don't have to stick to that.

The quick alternative for an energizing breakfast: Greens.

The easiest way to get plenty of greens? Smoothies... the simplest, most delicious invention for getting your quota of fruits, vegetables and leafy things.

If you don't already have one, go get a blender. Now. It will be one of the best kitchen investments you will ever make (besides your food processor—and if you're willing to spend a chunk more, you can buy one that combines the two).

Once you have a dependable blender, you are only limited by your creativity. As soon as you get used to kick starting your day with a kale and ginger drink, you will find smoothies sneaking their way into other parts of your life. Low energy in the afternoon? There's a smoothie for that. On the verge of getting a cold? There's a smoothie for that too.

Morning Green Drink

Ingredients

4 stalks of kale, stems removed
1/2 apple
1/2 pear
juice of one lemon
chopped fresh ginger
1/2 - 1 cup (120-240 milliliters) water (depending on what
consistency you want)

Preparation

Put all ingredients in blender and mix until desired consistency.

MORE INGREDIENTS TO PLAY WITH

Fruits & berries: Pineapple, strawberries, blueberries, rasp-
berries, watermelon, bananas, pomegranate*
Liquids: Coconut milk or coconut water, rice milk, yogurt
Greens: Parsley, cabbage, spinach
Other: Chia seeds, ginger, nut butters (peanut and almond
butter work wonders)

*Blend by itself first, then strain out the seeds, then add other ingredients

STOCKING YOUR PANTRY

If we're not willing to settle for junk living, we certainly
shouldn't settle for junk food.
–Sally Edwards

When people tell me they don't like to cook, I look at their pantry. More often than not, there is a crusty old container of salt, a half used bag of pasta and, if you're lucky, some item of canned food that wouldn't even cut it for a Thanksgiving casserole. I wouldn't want to cook either.

Then there are the people who love to cook. On a recent visit to see a friend, she pointed to one cabinet door and said, "the tea and chocolate is in there." I opened the door up to an extensive collection of teas, dark chocolate and whole grains in mason jars.

In the kitchen, you have to stay inspired, even—especially— if it's just for a simple dinner of quinoa and Brussels sprouts. Making food is like creating a work of art. Imagine if you had to go out and buy a pen, a pencil and a drawing pad every time you wanted to sketch. You wouldn't do it. Keeping a pantry stocked with the essentials is the first step in learning how to cook better and at the same time, to enjoy it.

It also comes down to budget; if you have to buy each individual ingredient for a recipe when you go to the store, you are going to get overwhelmed. It's taxing on your senses and your wallet, not to mention that you'll be weighed down with more goods when you bike home. Build up the pantry so you can start shopping in smaller amounts.

Every ingredient in a recipe serves a purpose, and it should be treated as such. Put those bulk grains in glass jars. Stock a pantry in a way that makes you happy. Because on those nights when you're out of greens and you haven't gone shopping in days, you want to be able to throw together a random assortment of quinoa and spices, and at the very least find a chocolate bar for dessert.

PANTRY ESSENTIALS

Quinoa: When all else fails, a bowl of quinoa, olive oil and sauteed kale will do for dinner.

Brown rice: Better than the white stuff, you can cook it on its own or add to salads and soups.

Oatmeal: For a heartier breakfast than usual, throw in a spoonful of peanut butter.

Pasta: Brown rice and quinoa are good versions for the gluten-free pantry

Flour: If you're stocking gluten-free flours, I like to keep them in the refrigerator.

Sugar: Keep both brown and organic cane sugar on hand.

Lentils: Like quinoa, lentils are an easy and quick meal. They also make for a great soup base.

Chickpeas: Add chickpeas to a salad or throw them into a stew for a little extra protein. You can also use them as dip bases and spreads like hummus.

Nutritional yeast: A vegan's dream ingredient, add it to popcorn and everything else you can think of. It's like magic.

Beans: Great Northern, Black or Kidney Beans are all good options for throwing together quick dinners. Just add quinoa or rice. Buy them in bulk and get in the habit of soaking overnight, or keep a few cans on hand for those times when you need something quick and easy.

Sea salt: You just don't ever want to be without sea salt.

Extra virgin olive oil: Good on anything and everything. Just make sure you get the good stuff and store in a cool, dark place.

Coconut oil: Switch it out for olive oil and butter.

Balsamic vinegar: Allows you to make a quick salad dressing.

Soy sauce: An easy way to add extra taste to any dish. It's always good to keep a gluten-free tamari version in the pantry as well.

Apple cider vinegar: Mix with olive oil and mustard for an easy vinaigrette.

Almonds: Eat them raw or grind them up into almond flour.

Walnuts: Full of omega 3s, and as good raw as they are roasted.

Honey: A natural sweetener that will also double as preventative care when you get a cold and need a warm cup of tea.

Coconut milk: Use it as a base for curries, or for an easy dessert, freeze with fresh berries.

Vegetable stock: Allows you to make a soup with not too many other ingredients on hand.

Peanut butter: Serve on apples, throw in with brown rice, vegetables and soy sauce for a simple peanut sauce or just eat it on a spoon.

Almond butter: Wouldn't want to get bored with the peanut version, right?

Dried fruit: Good for a snack and for adding to baked goods or serving with nuts.

Dark chocolate: Why would you ever want to be out of dark chocolate?

Tea: Keep an equal amount of black and green tea on hand.

Coffee: If you have ever run out of coffee, you know the pain of having to leave the house early in the morning in search of some.

Quinoa Apple Spice Cake

Ingredients

1 cup (6.25 ounces, 175 grams) quinoa, uncooked
1 cup (4.25 ounces, 120 grams) buckwheat flour
1 teaspoon baking powder
1 teaspoon baking soda
1 teaspoon sea salt
1/2 cup (3.5 ounces, 100 grams)
    organic sugar
1 teaspoon ground cinnamon
1 teaspoon ground ginger
1/2 teaspoon ground nutmeg
3 eggs
1/3 cup (80 milliliters) olive oil
1 teaspoon pure vanilla extract
1 large organic apple, peeled and diced

Preparation

Preheat oven to 350°F (175°C).

Bring 2 cups (480 milliliters) of water to a boil. Add quinoa and a dash of salt and let simmer for 12-15 minutes, or until water has cooked off. Remove from stove and set aside.

Mix dry ingredients.

Whisk eggs until frothy, then add in olive oil and vanilla extract. Add to dry mixture.

Combine all ingredients, including quinoa, and stir in apple pieces.

Grease a 9-inch round pan with olive oil. Pour batter in and bake for 30-40 minutes, until knife inserted into center comes out clean.

This recipe tastes great with a multitude of extras thrown in. Play around with a handful of chocolate chips and some dried figs, or add candied ginger for an extra kick.

EATING LOCALLY AND SEASONALLY

You don't have to cook fancy or complicated masterpieces—just good food from fresh ingredients.
–*Julia Child*

We would all like to pride ourselves on the fact that we eat locally and in season. But open your refrigerator. That soy sauce? I bet it wasn't produced anywhere near you. The candied ginger you're hoarding in your pantry for a late night snack? Certainly not from down the street.

When it comes to eating seasonally and locally, choose your battles. Find the balance between a strict winter diet of root vegetable soups and eating eight tropical fruits on a daily basis. That said, we could all do with thinking a little bit more about where our food comes from. Challenge yourself to find as many ingredients as possible that come from nearby. US-grown oranges might not come from near where you live, but they are better than the ones transported from farther away.

Some ways to incorporate more local and seasonal foods into your diet:

FORAGE

Do like your ancestors did and get back to the land. From seaweed to mushrooms, there are plenty of opportunities to get your hands dirty and pick food from the source. Just make sure you are abiding by appropriate laws and regulations and ensuring that you are not collecting poisonous items.

LOOK AT LABELS

This might seem simple, but often we're so focused on checking off our grocery list that we become semi-conscious consumers. Look at the label, think about where the product comes from, and if it's from the hinterlands of the other side of the world, think about an alternative ingredient. You might not be switching out your Rwandan coffee beans anytime soon, but perhaps you could commit to no more green bananas from Ecuador.

GET TO KNOW YOUR FARMER

If you have access to a local farmers market, hop on your bike and go. And don't just peruse, engage with the producers. They are the ones that know the growing season best. And if you're not sure what to do with a rutabaga, they will tell you. Find out if there is a CSA (Community Supported Agriculture) program near you, which lets you subscribe to a portion of a local farm's harvest every week during the growing season.

EXPLORE

You may be surprised at how many local and seasonal products are available to you. Sure, you may have never used them before, but this is the moment for culinary creativity. Put new ingredients to good use. Find new producers. Track down locally-made honey. Ask where you can buy fresh eggs. Not only are you engaging with your community in a new way, but you are finding alternative methods of putting a meal together, and there's a simple beauty in that.

PICNIC PLANNING

⚜

Things look different from the seat of a bike carrying a
sleeping bag with a cold beer tucked inside.
–Jim Malusa

An afternoon ride in the early spring sunshine followed by a picnic? Is there anything better in life? Eating outside is special for a reason: it's simple. It boils everything down to the essential elements. A basic meal. A good view. An interesting conversation. Outdoors, food is at its most basic. It's not necessarily about complicated creations, it's just about eating a meal in a beautiful setting, which often means that the meal itself doesn't even matter that much at all.

Outdoor eating experiences are a wonderful thing with even the most elementary ingredients. Pulling out a bit of cheese and an apple on an overlook can be way more meaningful than a five course dinner. Food is of course a holistic process, an experience that requires all of the senses. What we eat is just as important as how we eat it and who we're with. But back to the picnic.

Bike picnics are beautiful because they can take minimal planning—throw a sandwich in your bag and go. Or they can be complex affairs planned far in advance—think a quaint outdoor tablecloth spread on the ground with a bottle of bubbles. Whatever the affair, here are some things you should never leave home without:

UTENSILS

A stainless steel reusable spork will take you far. Or have a complete set of utensils (fork, knife, spoon) ready to throw in your bag at any occasion. You never know when the desire to picnic will strike.

A TEA TOWEL OR TABLECLOTH

A picnic on the bare ground is outdoorsy. A picnic on the ground with a tablecloth is classy. It doesn't have to be big - in fact a tea towel will do - but find something that can be your go-to piece of fabric to put on the ground and spread out your culinary delights on.

A GOOD KNIFE

The culinary cyclist should never be without a good knife. If you're just looking to cut an apple and slice cheese, a classic Opinel should do the trick, but if wine bottles are in your future, make sure you invest in a Swiss Army.

REUSABLE, DURABLE CUPS

You have to serve the bubbles in something. Stainless steel will take you far, and unless you are planning on hurling your cups off of a cliff, will most likely never break (or rust!). If you're up for it though, there's nothing quite like drinking out of real glass, so learn how to pack your flutes well. This is where the tea towel comes in handy: wrap your flutes individually, and for some extra protection use one of your extra layers that you were already planning on taking in case the weather changes mid-picnic.

THERMOS

Coffee—or any other warm libation—is always an excellent addition to the end of a picnic, or even a morning ride. The money you invest in a thermos is money saved at the coffee shop, and those disposable cups and lids that you won't have to use add up. Just make sure your thermos has a good seal to avoid coffee dribbling in your bag.

PICNIC MENU IDEAS

Simple: Brie + apple + baguette

Moderate: Carrots + hummus + goat cheese + avocado + bread + chocolate

Advanced: Quinoa salad + roasted veggie skewers + chocolate cake + espresso with cardamom

The Perfect Quinoa Picnic Salad with Mustard Citrus Vinaigrette

Ingredients

1/2 cup (3 ounces, 85 grams) white quinoa, uncooked
1/2 cup (3 ounces, 85 grams) red quinoa, uncooked
3 large carrots, thinly sliced
1 yellow pepper, diced
1/2 cup (2.5 ounces, 75 grams) dates, chopped
1/2 cup (2.25 ounces, 65 grams) walnuts
mixed salad greens
2 to 3 tablespoons chopped basil

Vinaigrette Ingredients

2 tablespoons olive oil
1 tablespoon apple cider vinegar
juice of 1/2 an orange
1 tablespoon Dijon mustard

Preparation

Place quinoa in a saucepan with 2 cups (480 milliliters) water and a pinch of sea salt and bring to a boil. Cover and let simmer for 12-15 minutes, or until water has cooked off. Set aside to cool.

In a large bowl, combine chopped carrots, dates, currants and walnuts.

For the vinaigrette, combine olive oil, apple cider vinegar and orange juice in a small jar or bowl. Add in mustard and whisk until well blended.

Toss quinoa with rest of salad ingredients and top with vinaigrette.

Before serving, mix in a couple of handfuls of mixed salad greens and garnish with basil.

DIY SNACK FOODS

⚬⬧⚬

Sugar is a type of bodily fuel, yes, but your body runs about
as well on it as a car would.
–*V.L. Allineare*

olive oil   fresh leaves   salt & pepper
              of kale

It's late, you're on your way home from work, and you bike past the grocery store on your commute home. You're hungry, and you're not really sure what's in your pantry, so you stop. Quickly the good intentions of finding something for dinner are taken over by a multitude of tasty gourmet snack products. Kale chips. Yes, please. A jar of Nutella? That could be considered dinner, right?

Soon you're in the checkout line, forking over way more cash than you intended to, and you're stuck lugging home a heavy backpack of goods on your bike.

Not anymore.

Two of my favorite snack foods are incredibly simple to make at home—and could almost be considered healthy.

Chocolate Hazelnut Spread

Ingredients

1 cup (5 ounces, 140 grams) roasted hazelnuts
1/4 cup (.75 ounces, 20 grams) cocoa powder
1/2 teaspoon flaky sea salt
2 tablespoons natural cane sugar
1 teaspoon almond extract
3 to 4 tablespoons canola oil or hazelnut oil, and more as
    needed

Preparation

Put all ingredients in food processor and mix until they are a spreadable consistency.

Pour into an airtight container and store in refrigerator.

Kale Chips

Ingredients

A bunch of kale
1-2 teaspoons of extra virgin olive oil
Flaky sea salt

Preparation

Preheat the oven to 375°F (190°C).

Rinse off the kale and remove the stems. Tear the strips into smaller pieces and put into a large mixing bowl.

Drizzle (lightly) with olive oil and add a few dashes of sea salt. Here is where you can get creative: add things like cumin, sesame seeds, parmesan cheese, maybe even a little Sriracha sauce for a different taste.

Spread out the kale on the baking sheet (you can put down a layer of parchment paper first for easier cleanup) and bake for 12-15 minutes or until the kale is slightly browned around the edges.

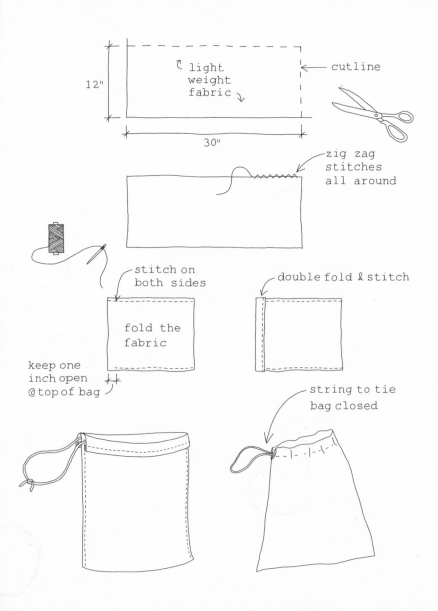

light weight fabric

cutline

12"

30"

zig zag stitches all around

stitch on both sides

double fold & stitch

fold the fabric

keep one inch open @ top of bag

string to tie bag closed

NAVIGATING THE BULK AISLE

❧⚜❧

One cannot think well, love well, sleep well, if one has not
dined well. –*Virginia Woolf*

You bike to the grocery store and you find yourself in the bulk section—that glorious place where everything seems possible. Ingredients as far as the eye can see, the potential for who knows what. But that is exactly the problem: what do you do with all of that stuff? We have all heard that we should be reaping the benefits of flaxseed, and am I not supposed to be doing something with chia seeds? We know we should be putting all this bulk goodness to use in one way or another, but how?

The key to mastering the largesse of the bulk aisle is to start small and work your way up. Try things that you have never tried before. Use a new ingredient in a recipe.

Plan ahead for the bulk aisle and bring your own bags. I like to keep a few plastic bags from previous bulk runs in all of my various backpacks that I use for biking so that I always have an option no matter where I am. Reusable cloth bags can be purchased, or you can sew your own using the pattern. Throw them in the washing machine between uses, and you're good to go.

Here's a suggested shopping list of bulk products to stock up on, and some tips on how to prepare them.

FLOURS & SUGAR

Yes! Buy them! Go crazy and buy an assortment. Baking is more fun when you are blending flours and not just sticking to one kind.

Unbleached pastry flour (or gluten-free equivalent)
Whole wheat flour
Brown rice flour
Organic cane sugar
Brown sugar

GRAINS (AND HOW TO COOK THEM)

Keep a few mason jars of various grains on hand and you will always have the foundation of a good meal, for breakfast or dinner.

Oatmeal: 1 part oatmeal to 3 parts liquid. For rolled regular or quick cooking: bring to boil with a little salt and then let simmer for 5-10 minutes.

Quinoa: 1 part quinoa to 2 parts liquid. Simmer covered for 15-20 minutes. Remove from heat and let sit for a few minutes.

Millet: 1 part millet to 2 1/2 parts liquid. Simmer covered 25-35 minutes.

Kasha: 1 part kasha to 2 parts liquid, or grind into buckwheat flour. Simmer for 15 minutes.

Lentils: 1 part lentils to 3 parts liquid. Bring water to boil, add lentils and simmer for 30-40 minutes.

Couscous: 1 part couscous to 2 parts liquid. Boil liquid and stir in couscous. Remove from heat and let sit until all liquid is absorbed.

SEEDS

Seeds are an easy and energizing snack, and can also be the base for making your own energy bars or granola (recipe below).

Seeds to buy in bulk: Sunflower, flax, pumpkin

NUTS

Buying raw nuts in bulk opens up your snacking and garnishing options. Try lightly roasting any of them with oil and spices. Or make nut butters (recipe below).

Nuts to buy in bulk: Almonds, walnuts, cashews, hazelnuts

DRIED FRUITS

Keep dried fruit on hand as a snack or to add to morning oatmeal.

Dried fruits to buy in bulk: Apricots, dates, figs, cherries, blueberries

OTHER

Shredded coconut: Good for adding to granola, or on top of cakes.

Spices: Buying spices in bulk is much cheaper and saves on packaging (see Essential Spices section)

Loose leaf tea: if you are lucky enough to live close to a store with bulk tea, dried herbs, and spices, you make your own blends.

(See the last chapter.)

Raw Walnut Butter with Honey and Sea Salt

Ingredients

2 cups (9 ounces, 260 grams) raw walnuts

3 tablespoons oil (go all out and get walnut oil, or if you're in a pinch use a flavorless oil like safflower)

2 tablespoons honey

1 teaspoon sea salt

Preparation

Put all ingredients in a food processor and grind until smooth. This butter has a thick consistency, like cookie dough.

Basic Granola

Ingredients

3 cups (10.5 ounces, 300 grams) rolled oats (gluten-free
   certified if you are going that route)

3/4 cups (2.25 ounces, 65 grams) unsweetened shredded
   coconut (optional)

1/2 cup (2.5 ounces, 70 grams) almonds, chopped

1/3 cup (80 milliliters) honey

2 tablespoons olive oil

1 teaspoon ground cinnamon

1 teaspoon ground ginger

1 teaspoon ground cardamom

1 teaspoon sea salt

About 1 cup (3-5 ounces, 85-140 grams) dried fruit of your
   choice (raisins, blueberries, cherries... get creative)

Preparation

Preheat oven to 325°F (160°C).

Combine all dry ingredients in a bowl.

In a saucepan, melt olive oil and honey and whisk together.
Pour over dry ingredients and mix until thoroughly coated.

Spread out evenly on a baking sheet and bake for 20-30 minutes,
stirring mixture every 10 minutes. Remove from oven and let
cool before putting in an airtight container for storage.

ESSENTIAL SPICES

You can easily improve any dish with a few interesting spices. Too much spice is worse than not enough, so use a little at first and taste as you add more.

Here are ten spices to always keep on hand—and how to use them.

Basil: If you can, get a basil plant for your kitchen and keep it growing. There is nothing better than fresh basil, and it's versatile enough that it can go from using in salads to adding as a cocktail garnish. Plus you can make your own pesto.

Cardamom: Good in both savory and sweet dishes, cardamom adds an exotic flavor to anything you make. Try adding a pinch to your morning coffee, or mixing a few teaspoons of it into a batch of cookies.

Cayenne Pepper: Cayenne can be sprinkled onto salads, blended into sauces, or put onto kale chips.

Cinnamon: Cinnamon is another spice that works well in savory and sweet dishes alike. Add a little to a mug of hot chocolate or sprinkle over roasted squash.

Coriander: An excellent addition to stews and soups, coriander is the name for the seeds of the plant that we English speakers refer to as cilantro.

Cumin: Saute onions in cumin and olive oil for a good base for a vegetable soup, or add it to dips like guacamole and hummus.

Ginger: Powdered ginger in your morning yogurt will add an extra zing, and it's perfect with a little soy sauce to add to a stir fry.

Nutmeg: Try switching out nutmeg for cinnamon in baking recipes, or add into a quiche.

Rosemary: There is no simpler meal than a pan of roasted vegetables drizzled in olive oil and sprinkled with rosemary.

Smoked Paprika: The smoky taste of this spice goes a long way, especially in dishes with feta cheese and olive oil. Also great on roasted potatoes with a little yogurt sauce on the side.

Cardamom Currant Scones

Ingredients

2 cups (9.5 ounces, 270 grams)
    brown rice flour
1/2 cup (1.75 ounces, 50 grams)
    finely ground almonds
1 tablespoon baking powder
3 tablespoons natural cane sugar
1 tablespoon sea salt
2 teaspoons ground cardamom
8 tablespoons coconut oil
2 eggs
1 cup (240 milliliters) coconut milk
3/4 cup (3.75 ounces, 105 grams) currants

cardamom

pods   seeds   seeds
inside
pod

Preparation

Preheat oven to 450°F (230°C).

Mix flour, ground almonds, baking powder, sugar, salt and cardamom. Add coconut oil and mix together until it resembles coarse meal. The easiest way to do this is in a food processor.

Whisk eggs in a small bowl. Set aside about 2 tablespoons of egg in a separate bowl for brushing on top of scones. Mix rest of eggs together with coconut milk.

Mix in the currants in the flour mixture and then add eggs and milk. Mix together until dough forms.

Make two round balls and flatten on greased baking pan. Cut each round into fourths and brush on remaining egg with a pastry brush.

Bake at 450°F (230°C) for 15 min.

Place on baking rack to cool.

TRANSPORTING YOUR FOOD

I only bike with a backpack. No panniers, no rear rack, no European-style front basket, no cargo bike. More elaborately equipped cyclists may pass judgment. But I'm only proof that to live a life on two wheels, you don't need a closet full of bike-only accessories. A trusty bicycle, your legs, and a bag to carry your goods in is a very nice start.

Transporting food via bicycle sometimes takes a bit of ingenuity and planning. If you're invited to a dinner party, don't commit to bringing a huge casserole straight out of the oven unless you own a cargo bike or a trailer.

I once overdid things and made a Dutch apple pie to take to a friend's house, completely forgetting to think about the transportation options. Too loose to put in the backpack sideways, I was stuck with one solution: tote bag. I am certain that the pie would have been more content with a bike and basket from its motherland, but I later learned that the "carefully hung tote bag" is in fact a well known way to transport food. The bag swings gently from your hand or handlebars, but your dish will stay upright. It just takes some careful balancing when you need to brake.

Here are some more useful tips on carrying groceries and foodstuffs on your bike.

PLAN, PLAN, PLAN

You're not just figuring out what you need to stock your refrigerator with, you are figuring out which groceries will fit into your bag. While making your grocery list, envision how much space everything will take up. When I am at the store, I stick to the 3/4 shopping basket rule: grab a little basket with handles rather than a wheeled cart, and make sure to only fill it 3/4 of the way full. If you have a larger backpack or panniers, you'll learn how much you can fill your basket through trial and error.

SHOP SMALL AND OFTEN

It might seem more time- and cost-effective to do a big grocery run every few weeks, but if you have the luxury of living close to a market, get in the habit of smaller shopping trips. This will allow you to eat more fresh produce and also minimize your overall food waste, as you'll be shopping for specific ingredients for specific meals and can better gauge the quantity of food that you actually need. That's how millions of Europeans shop.

AVOID EXCESSIVE PACKAGING

Not every item of produce needs to be put in an individual bag. If you buy in bulk, not only will you avoid a lot of single-use plastic, but you'll maximize on your carrying space.

KEEP AN ONGOING GROCERY LIST WITH YOU

It's easy to make a quick stop at the grocery store on the way home from work or elsewhere, so it's good to keep an ongoing list of the essentials that you keep on hand at home and when you run out of them. If you're big on using your smartphone, there are good apps for such things, but you can also keep a small journal in your bag with a list of the twenty or so most basic things you tend to buy and keep on hand—think, peanut butter, yogurt, kale—to remind yourself when you are out at the store.

KEEP THE GREENS FOR LAST

Ever seen someone biking with kale sticking out of their bag? There's no better sight. Keep the leafy greens aside when you are packing your groceries and put them in at the end; this will save them from being squished and save you space, as you can let them stick out of your bag a bit.

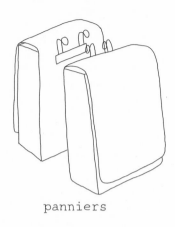

panniers

water bottle holder

rear carrier rack

waterproof backpack

front basket
(removable)

front basket
(fixed)

bungee cord

crate basket

front mounting

Dutch Apple Pie with Cardamom

This recipe is intended for a 9-inch springform pan, resulting in a very big pie. If you're using a smaller pan, you may want to cut the recipe in half, or bake two pies.

Crust Ingredients

1 cup butter (8 ounces, 225 grams) butter
3/4 cup (5.25 ounces, 150 grams) natural cane sugar
1 cup (4.75 ounces, 135 grams) rice flour
1 cup (4.25 ounces, 120 grams) buckwheat flour
2 cups (7 ounces, 200 grams) almond meal or finely ground almonds
2 teaspoons baking powder
2 large eggs, lightly whisked
1 teaspoon ground cardamom

Filling Ingredients

8 to 10 small to medium apples (about 2 pounds, 900 grams)
1/2 cup (3.75 ounces, 105 grams) brown sugar
1/2 cup (2.5 ounces, 70 grams) raisins
juice + zest of 1/2 lemon or orange
1 teaspoon ground cinnamon
1 teaspoon ground cardamom
1 teaspoon ground nutmeg

Preparation

Preheat the oven to 400°F (200°C).

Start by preparing the crust. Cream butter and sugar and set aside. In a separate bowl, mix together all dry crust ingredients.

Add eggs to the butter and sugar mixture, saving about 1 tablespoon of whisked eggs to top the crust with before baking. Add in the flour mixture and work together with your hands until the dough forms into a ball. Cover and chill in the refrigerator while you prepare the filling.

Peel and quarter all of the apples and cut into small, bite-sizes pieces. Mix in rest of ingredients until apples are evenly coated with spices.

Grease a 9-inch springform pan. Set aside about 1/4 of the crust, and place the rest in the bottom of the pan. Push out until the bottom and sides of pan are completely covered. Fill with apple mixture. Roll out the remaining crust into a circle, or press out with your hands, and place on top of the pie, pinching together the top of the crust to the sides. Brush the top with the tablespoon of egg and sprinkle with brown sugar.

Bake for 45-50 minutes.

Serve by itself or in the classic Dutch style, with whipped cream.

FEEDING YOUR VEGAN AND GLUTEN-FREE FRIENDS

⤜⤛

If you really want to make a friend, go to someone's house and eat with him... the people who give you their food give you their heart.
–*Cesar Chavez*

In this day and age most of us have one dietary restriction or another. Be it for health, ethical or simply personal reasons, we live in a world where we can meticulously choose what we eat. Either we're off nightshades, on a goat's milk only diet, or free from all carbohydrates. Without launching into the nuances of how we choose what we eat and the social implications of such, I will say one thing: when it comes to modern food etiquette, the host has to be just as accommodating as the invitee.

Serving food to others is a matter of social grace and it is important to know what your dinner guests can and can't consume. This of course should not stop you from making your preferred pièce de resistance, but knowing your crowd is the indicator of a good host or hostess. Thinking out of the box will get you far more points than sticking to a set menu. Plus it also allows you to launch into new cuisines you may never have attempted otherwise.

SOME EASY OPTIONS FOR THE VEGAN DINNER PARTY

Flaxseed crackers with tapenade
Quinoa stuffed squash
Roasted vegetables
Anything with avocado

But then we get to everything beyond the dinner table. What about baked goods? Snacks? Let's remember one thing about food: just like cycling, it should be fun. So when someone has a dietary restriction or preference, let it not be a hindrance but an opportunity for creativity. Play around. You might just end up with something that was better than the original.

BASIC SUBSTITUTES FOR REGULAR INGREDIENTS

Butter: Coconut oil, avocade puree, banana, olive oil, applesauce

Flour: Rice flour, almond meal, polenta, ground nuts, oat flour, buckwheat, coconut flour

Sugar: Molasses, banana, fruit juice, applesauce, maple syrup

Eggs: Chia seeds (1 tablespoon + 3 tablespoons warm water); ground flax seeds (1 tablespoon + 3 tablespoons warm water); vinegar (1 teaspoon baking powder + 1 tablespoon water + 1 tablespoon vinegar)

The important thing to remember about substitutes is that the quantities won't always be the same, particularly when it comes to flours. Go slowly, don't be afraid to mess up, and be ready for those unintended moments of culinary serendipity.

Olive Oil and Polenta Cake

Ingredients

3 eggs

1/2 cup (3.5 ounces, 100 grams) natural cane sugar

3/4 cup (6 ounces, 170 grams) butter (coconut oil is a good substitute, for your vegan friends)

3/4 cup (4.25 ounces, 120 grams) cornmeal

1 cup (3.5 ounces, 100 grams) almond meal or finely ground almonds

1 teaspoon baking powder

3 tablespoons olive oil

1 teaspoon sea salt

juice and zest of 1 Meyer lemon

zest of 1/2 an orange

Preparation

Preheat oven to 350°F (175°C).

Beat eggs in a bowl and add sugar.

In another bowl combine dry ingredients.

In a saucepan melt butter. Add to egg and sugar batter and add in dry ingredients. Mix in rest of ingredients.

Pour batter into a greased 9-inch baking pan and bake for 20-25 minutes, until golden brown.

Let cool and dust with powdered sugar if you're feeling super fancy.

Five Seed Crackers with Olive Tapenade

CRACKERS

Ingredients

1 (240 milliliters) cup water
1 cup (5.25 ounces, 150 grams) raw flax seeds
1/2 cup (2.25 ounces, 65 grams) raw pumpkin seeds
1/2 cup (2.75 ounces, 75 grams) raw sesame seeds
1/2 cup (2.5 ounces, 70 grams) raw sunflower seeds
1/2 cup (2.5 ounces, 70 grams) raw hazelnuts, finely chopped
1 teaspoon cumin powder
1 teaspoon sea salt

Preparation

Combine water and flax seeds in a bowl and let sit for three hours.

Mix in rest of ingredients and let sit for an additional hour.

Preheat oven to 300°F (150°C).

Spread out the mixture onto a lined baking sheet (a silicone baking mat works great for this) and bake for 45 minutes.

Reduce the heat to 230°F (110°C) and open oven door to let out steam. Bake for another 15-30 minutes and open door again. Check how crispy the crackers are by breaking off a corner. If they still feel soft, beak for an additional 15-30 minutes.

Let cool, and then break into pieces. You will find that you will get some small crumbles. Keep those on hand for sprinkling over salad or your morning yogurt.

Store in an airtight container.

TAPENADE

Ingredients

1 6-ounce can (170 grams) organic black olives
1/2 of a roasted red pepper, chopped
1 tablespoon olive oil
1/2 cup (2.5 ounces, 70 grams) raw almonds
1 teaspoon sea salt
1 teaspoon rosemary or Herbes de
    Provence
1/2 teaspoon black pepper

Preparation

Mix all ingredients in food processor
until well blended. Store in airtight container in refrigerator.

❧❦❧

Then there are times when all you want is comfort food; easy to make, easy to eat. You've ridden home in a downpour. It's Saturday night and you're curling up on the couch with a movie. You're feeling a little down and all you want is macaroni and cheese. It's during those moments that I bust out the I-Can-Do-Anything Kale and Garlic Vegan Cream Sauce.

This sauce is hard to describe, because it really can do anything. It can go from salad dressing to dip to pasta sauce. My preferred method of eating it is over a plate of roasted vegetables, but it's also the ideal addition to a bowl of quinoa or brown rice pasta when you need to carbo load or deal with a comfort food craving. It keeps for about a week in the refrigerator, which makes it the perfect thing to have on hand when you need dinner in a pinch.

The I-Can-Do-Anything Kale and Garlic Vegan Cream Sauce

Ingredients

1 cup (4 ounces, 115 grams) raw cashews + 1 cup (240 milliliters) water for soaking
1 cup (240 milliliters) water
3-4 large kale leaves, chopped and with stem removed
1-2 garlic cloves (depends on how punchy you want this to be - if you want a smoother taste, roast the garlic first)
dash of sea salt + black pepper
lemon juice to taste (optional)

Note: Don't have kale? Parsley is an excellent substitute. Use about a cup (2 ounces, 60 grams) of chopped leaves.

Preparation

Soak cashews in 1 cup (240 milliliters) water for at least one hour. Drain.

In a blender or food processor, combine drained cashews, kale leaves and garlic. Add the rest of the water. Puree until you get a smooth consistency.

Store in an airtight container in the refrigerator.

THE ART OF GIFTING FOOD

Cooking is like love. It should be entered into with abandon
or not at all.
–*Harriet van Horne*

Mason jars. The ultimate in any culinary cyclist's gift giving repertoire.

Your mother always told you that handmade gifts were better. What she may have forgotten to add was that handmade food gifts are better. A jam, a batch of granola, spiced nuts... you are only limited by what you are willing to make. The right size mason jar can fit in your bicycle's water bottle cage, which means gift giving on the go.

Marmalade is always a food gift that goes over well, mostly because it's easy to make and everyone loves having a jar of homemade confiture in their refrigerator. This one puts carrots and cardamom to use—sure to impress the recipient but easy enough to make in an afternoon.

Cardamom Carrot Marmalade

Ingredients

2 cups (about 6.5 ounces, 180 grams) grated carrots
2 cups (480 milliliters) water
2 cups (14 ounces, 400 grams) natural cane sugar
zest + juice of one Meyer lemon
zest + juice of one orange
3 teaspoons green cardamom pods
1 teaspoon cardamom seeds, ground (I take whole cardamom
    seeds and grind them in a coffee grinder or mortar and
    pestle - you get larger bits of cardamom by doing this,
    which make this recipe extra good)

Preparation

In a saucepan, combine the water, cardamom pods and juice +
zest of the lemon and orange. Bring the water to a boil and let
simmer for about 15 minutes. Remove from heat and take out
the cardamom pods with a spoon.

Add in carrots and sugar and simmer for about 35-45 minutes,
constantly stirring, until marmalade has thickened.

Pour into a clean jar. Store in the refrigerator.

If the marmalade is too loose once it has set, cook it down
longer. If it is too hard, just put it back in the saucepan with
1/4 to 1/2 cup (60 to 120 milliliters) water, warming until the
marmalade loosens, then simmer until you get the consistency
you want.

THE BICYCLE-FRIENDLY
HOME BAR

❧✿❧

Wine to me is passion. It's family and friends. It's
warmth of heart and generosity of spirit. Wine is art.
It's culture. It's the essence of civilization and the art of
living.
–*Robert Mondavi*

The culinary cyclist wants drinks that are easy to make and to transport. Whether it's in a flask or your committed cocktail reusable drinking vessel, keeping a few things on hand at home means that you can serve up a drink when friends drop by after work or brew up a concoction to drag along on your evening excursion.

Here is a quick guide to six different libations and what to do with them.

Whiskey: A classic that works mixed with a good ginger ale (homemade of course!) or just by itself in the flask. Be sure to have both Bourbon and Scotch - you always want to be able to offer someone a nice stiff after dinner drink on the rocks.

Gin: Did someone say gin and tonic? Or get fancy and mix with a homemade lemonade and club soda.

Rum: If you want to drink it straight, keep the dark stuff on hand. If you are more of a mixer, opt for something lighter.

Tequila: Lime, sugar, tequila, go.

Craft Beer: It is important to always keep a good craft beer on hand, no matter what the occasion. Just buy the size that fits in your water bottle cage.

Wine: Always bring a bottle when you are invited to a dinner. Always. Don't be afraid of being a wine expert. Ask questions. Find a varietal that you like. Experiment with pairing. Remember that wine, just like food, should be fun. Make it so.

Other stuff: Tonic water, club soda, ginger ale, lime and lemons.

Homemade Ginger Ale

Ingredients

1 cup (240 milliliters) honey or 1 cup (7 ounces, 200 grams) natural sugar
1 cup (5.5 ounces, 160 grams) sliced and peeled ginger
1 cup (240 milliliters) water

Preparation

To make syrup: Put all ingredients in a saucepan and bring to a simmer. Cook for about 15 minutes until all honey or sugar has dissolved and you get a strong ginger smell. Let cool. Strain syrup into a bottle and store in refrigerator.

To make the ginger ale, combine syrup with with club soda (start with a 1 to 4 ratio, and then adjust depending on how strong you want it). Add whiskey and a sprig of mint, rosemary or basil if you're feeling like a classy cocktail.

HOSTING A DINNER PARTY

We should look for someone to eat and drink with before
looking for something to eat and drink.
–Epicurus

So much of eating is social—and what better way to bring people together than around a meal? For many, however, hosting a dinner party can be overwhelming.

Stick to some key rules for successful hosting and you'll avoid that overwhelmed feeling and instead be able to focus on all the good things that eating with other people can bring. Good friends around a table of good food—what's to be afraid of?S

SMALLER IS BETTER

For dinner party novices, stick to a variety of small plates, tapas style. This allows you to play around in the kitchen (and prepare things in advance) and provides your guests a diverse sampling of foods. It also means that if you mess one of them up, there are still plenty more to try.

AVOID ANY COMPLETELY NEW RECIPE

By all means, branch out, but make sure that an element of the recipe that you're attacking is something you have done before. There is nothing worse then being in over your head fifteen minutes before guests arrive.

ASK GUESTS TO HELP

Unless you're going full on and pairing wines with your appetizer, entree, and dessert (which you should certainly feel empowered to do), it is always appropriate to ask guests to bring a bottle of wine. In fact, good guests will bring a bottle of wine without being asked—keep that in mind when you are invited somewhere.

ALWAYS HAVE AN APPETIZER

It doesn't have to be complicated, but having a little amuse-bouche is always a good thing—preferably paired with a pre-dinner drink, of course. A great go-to is goat cheese with walnuts and honey.

Place goat cheese in a ovenproof dish, drizzle with honey, top with chopped walnuts and place in the oven until melted. Serve with bread or crackers. Tastes fancy, but can be made within seconds of the guests showing up.

TIMING IS EVERYTHING

If you don't think about what dishes are going to be served when and at what time, you will run into that classic dilemma of hot food that's lukewarm. Make a list of what you are planning on cooking and figure out in what order you are going to prepare them.

USE REAL DISHES

The goal here is to be classy. No one wants to be served dinner on a paper plate. No one. Unless you're at a barbeque, and even then you should encourage people to bring their own reusable plates and cutlery.

WOW YOUR GUESTS

Always have at least one "kill it" dish on the menu. You know what I'm talking about. The one dish that you are never going to mess up. That way, when all else goes to hell you still have something good to serve.

OWN IT

Julia Child had a policy of never apologizing for culinary mishaps. Even if you completely destroy a dish, don't make excuses. It is far more awkward for your guests to respond "no no, it's amazing!" when you profusely apologize for your burnt soup. Just whisk the soup away and bring out dessert and nobody will mind a bit.

THE BASIC
CHOCOLATE CAKE

৵৻৵

Let's face it, a nice creamy chocolate cake
does a lot for a lot of people; it does for me.
–Audrey Hepburn

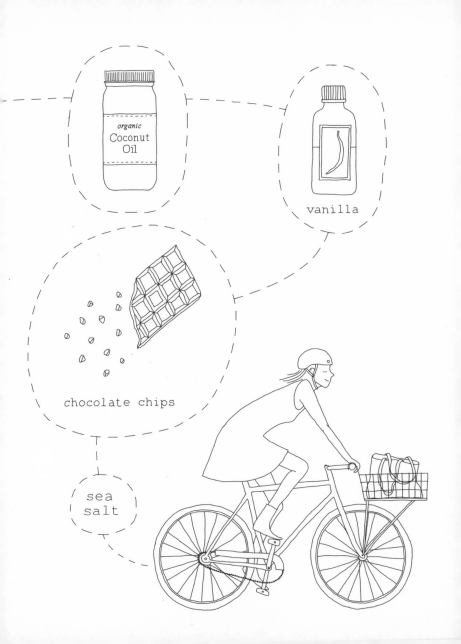

When you're invited to dinner somewhere, you want to have a recipe that you can whip up quickly. No one wants to spend hours in the kitchen prepping something to take along to a dinner, only to have it collapse in the 30 minutes before you have to leave. Plus, when you are biking to said dinner party you need something that's going to be portable. Enter this chocolate cake.

Chocolate cake is the defining factor in a cook's repertoire. It's one of those basic dishes that if you master it, you'll be known for it. You'll get asked to bring it to get-togethers with friends. You'll find yourself baking it on a Sunday night because you just happen to have all of the ingredients on hand. After all, a Chocolate Sea Salt Cake baking adventure on Sunday night means Chocolate Sea Salt Cake for breakfast on Monday morning.

What makes this cake ideal for the culinary cyclist is not just that it's easy, but that because it's so dense, it's easy to transport. Once it's baked, the cake and the cake pan can be slid into a plastic bag for protection and placed in a backpack. Note that this cake is best the day after you have baked it, which means that it's ideal for wrapping a few slices in aluminum foil and taking with you so you can have a pick-me-up in the afternoon work lull.

This one was inspired by a classic Swedish recipe (referred to in Swedish as "sticky cake" because it's meant to be almost undercooked), altered by Johanna Kindvall, and altered yet again by myself. The original recipe calls for cocoa powder, but I find that using chocolate chips gives it a denser consistency, almost like eating a cake-like chocolate bar. It has been tweaked to be dairy-free, but feel free to use butter instead of coconut oil.

Chocolate Sea Salt Cake

Ingredients

2 eggs

1/4 cup (1.75 ounces, 50 grams) natural cane sugar

3/4 cup (2.75 ounces, 75 grams) almond meal or finely ground
almonds

1/4 cup (1.25 ounces, 35 grams) rice flour

8 tablespoons coconut oil

3/4 cup (4.25 ounces, 120 grams) chocolate chips or finely
chopped dark chocolate

1 teaspoon pure vanilla extract

1 teaspoon sea salt

coarse sea salt and chocolate chips or finely chopped dark
chocolate for garnish

Preparation

Preheat oven to 350°F (175°C).

In a bowl, whisk eggs. Add in sugar and whisk until well
blended. Add in almond meal and rice flour.

In a saucepan, melt coconut oil and chocolate on low heat. Add
to rest of mixture.

Pour into a greased and floured 9-inch cake pan. (If you're
making this for gluten-free friends be sure you are flouring with
rice flour or almond meal.)

Bake for 12-15 minutes. Remove from oven and sprinkle with
chocolate chips. Put back in oven for about two more minutes.
Remove from oven, and with a knife or spatula, carefully spread
out melted chocolate chips so that they cover the cake.

Sprinkle with sea salt and serve.

BLEND YOUR OWN TEA

❧

To the right, books; to the left, a tea-cup. In front of me, the fireplace; behind me, the post. There is no greater happiness than this.

–Teiga

We started this book with coffee, and it only makes sense to end it with tea. Coffee wakes us up and opens us up to the world; tea draws us back in, grounds us, and gives us pause for reflection.

Think of curling up on a couch with a mug of tea. It's the drink for when you need to relax, take a deep breath, and end your day. It's one mindset of simple living—all you need to live well is a big mug and a good book.

And a good recipe for tea.

Much like coffee, there is a craft to good tea, and tea connoisseurs can go on for hours about tea plantations, infusions, and the ultimate teapot.

A lot of tea experimentation can be done at home. All it takes is some bulk tea leaves and a little creativity. My favorite pairing is an Earl Gray Lavender tea, discovered in a small cafe in Banff, Canada and later made at home when I eventually ran out.

Earl Grey Lavender Tea

Ingredients

3-6 lavender buds (if not plucking from your own yard, make
    sure to get culinary grade)
1 teaspoon Earl Grey tea leaves

Preparation

Boil water and let tea steep for about 4 minutes or so.

Increase the amounts of lavender and tea leaves if you want
to make a bigger batch to keep on hand. Store in an airtight
container.

Here are some more pairings to guide you:
Black Tea: Cinnamon, cardamom, ginger, peppercorns, rose
    petals, vanilla beans, dried berries, cacao nibs
Green Tea: Citrus peels (like Meyer Lemon, grapefruit or
    blood orange), fennel seeds, licorice, mint, lemongrass,
    matcha
Rooiboos: Saffron, cacao nibs, ginger, mint, orange peel

And because it's always nice to have a little treat with your evening cup of tea, try these simple peanut butter cookies.

Peanut Butter Cookies

Ingredients

1 cup (9 ounces, 255 grams) crunchy, salted peanut butter

1/3 cup (2 ounces, 70 grams) natural cane sugar

1 egg, lightly beaten (if you want to make these vegan, switch out for 1 tablespoon ground flax seeds and 3 tablespoons warm water)

1 teaspoon pure vanilla extract

1/3 cup (1.75 ounces, 50 grams) chocolate chips or finely chopped dark chocolate

Preparation

Preheat oven to 350°F (175°C).

In a bowl, combine egg, sugar, and vanilla extract. Add in peanut butter and chocolate chips and stir together.

Scoop out about a tablespoon of dough and roll into a ball. Place on greased baking sheet and flatten carefully with a fork.

Bake for 12-16 minutes.

Let sit for a few minutes before transferring them to a cooling rack.

Now go enjoy a day well lived.

bits of
chocolate

peanut butter
cookie

EP I LOGUE

～✦～

The bicycle, the bicycle surely, should always be the vehicle
of novelists and poets.
–*Christopher Morley*

This book started on a Peugeot in Portland and ended on a Vélib in Paris, two cities that embrace food and bikes.

Portland is my grounding place, yet Paris promised new adventures and an infusion of creativity. I had to write, and it seemed the perfect place to do so. So I went.

In a city that's familiar, you know its ins and outs like you know the back of your hand. You know which detour to take, which route to go when you need something more scenic. You find beauty in your routine. In a new city you discover the places that will later become part of your everyday, attacking them with a kind of fervor and intent that comes from falling in love with something new. You explore, you learn and soon novelties turn into everyday habits. What was once foreign and unknown—a street, a metro stop, a cafe—becomes a part of you. You embrace it, internalize it and make it your own.

In Portland, I know my bike routes routes and cycling is easy. In Paris, I had to learn to navigate all over again. Dodging scooters, identifying the streets with separated bike lanes and constantly laying on the bell so as to not run over pedestrians. Conquering all of that was beautiful, taking me out of my comfort zone and making me fall in love with cycling all over again.

Food is the same. We ground ourselves in our staples and return to our comfort foods when we seek solace. Yet we also explore new ingredients and jump into the unknown of new recipes.

This book was written out of a love of eating, riding and adventure. I hope that you have found some inspiration in it, be it a recipe, an idea or just a moment to reflect on your own eating habits, and ultimately, that you have enjoyed reading it as much as I enjoyed writing it.

Here's to sunny bike rides and early morning French presses.

—Anna Brones Paris, 2013

About the author

Anna Brones is a writer and producer with a love for travel, good food and the outdoors. She runs the website Foodie Underground where she posts weekly recipes and is a regular contributor to Sprudge and The Kitchn. Her work has been featured in The Guardian, BBC, Slate, The New York Times and more. She has ridden many different bicycles in her life, everywhere from Portland to Paris to Amsterdam to Yogyakarta.

About the illustrator

Johanna Kindvall is an illustrator whose work has been featured in various books and magazines, including The Fabulous Baker Brothers by Tom & Henry Herbert and Art of Eating. Her work also includes graphics for the web and packaging and pattern designs for fabrics and wallpaper. As a serious home cook and editor of her illustrated cooking site, Kokblog (started in 2005) many of her drawings are food related. Johanna is based in Brooklyn and the south of Sweden. She rides a chrome single speed bicycle with coaster brakes.

Anna and Johanna also collaborated on the illustrated cookbook *Fika: The Art of the Swedish Coffee Break* (Spring 2015, Ten Speed Press), with recipes and stories inspired by their Swedish roots.

RECIPE INDEX

Recipes are marked V for vegan and GF for gluten-free. Sometimes the recipes allow for vegan or gluten-free options within the recipe, so be sure to pay attention!

MORE TITLES

Pedal, Stretch, Breathe: The Yoga of Bicycling

by Kelli Refer, $9.95

Let this unique book help you feel more calm and limber on and off the bicycle in all seasons. Refer, a yoga instructor and daily bike rider, guides you through stretches for your knees, hips, and back, shows you breathing exercises to get you up hills, and introduces you to the elements of yoga philosophy.

Bikes in Space: A Feminist Science Fiction Anthology, Vol 1-3

Edited by Elly Blue, $9.95 each

In the first anthology of its kind, a variety of authors bring you their two-wheeled visions of the future. Some are whimsical, some are bleak, all are entertaining, thought-provoking, and feature inspiring female main characters.

Our Bodies, Our Bikes

Edited by Elly Blue & April Streeter, $14.95

A big book of of personal stories interspersed with expertise and advice on wellness, sexuality, body image, training, recovery, childbirth, bike fit, ability, and much more. An indispensable reference for anyone who rides a bicycle and has a body.

SUBSCRIBE TO EVERYTHING WE PUBLISH!

Do you love what Microcosm publishes?

Do you want us to publish more great stuff?

Would you like to receive each new title as it's published?

Subscribe as a BFF to our new titles and we'll mail them all to you as they are released!

$10-30/mo, pay what you can afford. Include your t-shirt size and month/ date of birthday for a possible surprise! Subscription begins the month after it is purchased.

microcosmpublishing.com/bff

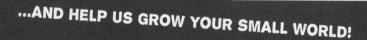